A to Z Greece

BY BYRON AND REBECCA AUGUSTIN

children's press®

A Division of Scholastic Inc.
New York Toronto London Auckland Sydney
Mexico City New Delhi Hong Kong
Danbury, Connecticut

Consultant: Dr. George Kourvetaris, Professor, Northern Illinois University, De Kalb, Illinois
Series Design: Marie O'Neill
Photo Research: Caroline Anderson
Language Consultant: Evans Mirageas

The photos on the cover show a pelican on Mykonos (top left), the Parthenon (top right),
a hand-painted reproduction of an ancient Greek vase (bottom right), and a young Greek boy
in traditional clothing (bottom center).

Photographs © 2005: akg-Images, London/Andrea Baguzzi: 17 right; Alamy Images/Tony Gervis/Rober
Harding Picture Library Ltd: 37 top; Bridgeman Art Library International Ltd., London/New York: 14 (Louvre,
Paris, France/Lauros/Giraudon), 13 (Pinacoteca Capitolina, Palazzo Conservatori, Rome, Italy/Giraudon);
Corbis Images: 12 bottom (ANA/Reuters), 8 (Owen Franken), cover bottom right (Dave Houser), 6 top
(Wolfgang Kaehler), 28 bottom (Yiorgos Karahalis/Reuters), 17 left (Leagros Group/Christie's Images), 34 bot-
tom (Francis G. Mayer), 26 (Gail Mooney), cover top left (Kevin Schafer), 33 (Ruben Sprich/Reuters), 5 top
(Hubert Stadler), 36 (Sandro Vannini), 37 bottom (Adam Woolfitt), 31; Danita Delimont Stock Photography/Jon
Arnold: 9 top; Digital Vision/Nicholas Pitt: 18; Getty Images: 7 left (Chris Hondros), cover center bottom (Will
& Deni McIntyre), cover top right (Antonio Rosario), 5 bottom (Stone), 15 left (Time Life Pictures); Index
Stock Imagery: 29 (Reid Neubert), 19 (Grayce Roessler); Landov, LLC/EPA: 28 top (Katia Christodoulou), 6
bottom (Louisa Gouliamaki); Lonely Planet Images: 25 bottom (Mark Daffey), 10 (Jon Davison), 23 (John Elk
III), 16 (Wayne Walton); Masterfile/Garry Black: 27 right; photolibrary.com/Bruce James: 11; Retrofile/PPP/
Popperfoto: 38; Superstock, Inc.: 25 top (Ping Amranand), 35 top (Bridgeman Art Library, London), 15 right
(Capitaline Museum, Rome); The Image Works: 35 bottom (AAAC/Topham), 24 (Bob Daemmrich), 9 bottom
(Margot Granitsas), 34 top (Jeff Greemberg), 7 right, 21 (A. Vossberg/VISUM); Tom Till Photography, Inc.: 22;
Transit Photo and Archive/Peter Hirth: 4; TRIP Photo Library: 27 left (Glyn Davies), 30 (V. Greaves), 12 top (B.
Turner), 32 (Bob Turner).
Map by XNR Productions, Inc.

Library of Congress Cataloging-in-Publication Data
Augustin, Byron.
  Greece / by Byron Augustin and Rebecca A. Augustin.
     p. cm. — (A to Z)
  Includes bibliographical references and index.
  ISBN 0-516-23664-4 (lib. bdg.)   0-516-24953-3 (pbk.)
  1. Greece—Juvenile literature. I. Augustin, Rebecca A. II. Title. III. Series.
  DF717.A875 2005
  949.5—dc22   2005006998

1 2 3 4 5 6 7 8 9 10 R 14 13 12 11 10 09 08 07 06 05

Contents

Goats thrive in the hilly, rocky Greek countryside.

Animals

Greece is home to a variety of wild animals, birds, and reptiles. There are also large herds of sheep and goats.

Herds of sheep have been a familiar sight in Greece for thousands of years.

Some of the common wild animals include foxes, deer, badgers, jackals, wild goats, and wild **boars.** Flocks of pelicans are found near fishing villages.

A small number of rare brown bears live in the rugged mountains of northern Greece. There are only about 120 brown bears left in the country. Laws prohibit hunting or killing these bears.

Pelican

Greek shepherds raise large herds of sheep and goats. These animals provide milk, meat, wool, and leather for their owners.

The Parthenon was built more than 2,000 years ago.

Olympic Stadium, Athens

Buildings

Greece has buildings that represent both ancient and modern architecture. The **Parthenon** was dedicated in 438 B.C. and was built of fine white marble. The Parthenon is located on the Acropolis, a hill overlooking the city of Athens.

The Olympic Stadium in Athens was the major site of the 2004 Summer Olympics. A beautiful steel and glass roof was added to the stadium for the Olympics. The stadium can seat 72,000 spectators.

Traffic jams are common in Athens.

With its historic sites, museums, galleries, hotels, and restaurants, crowded Athens is a popular tourist destination.

Cities

Athens is the capital of and most important city in Greece. More than 3 million people live in Athens. This is almost one-third of the nation's population.

Athens is a bustling center of factories, markets, offices, apartments, and luxury **villas.** Drivers in cars and buses speed through the streets honking their horns. Traffic congestion and air pollution are major problems.

Greek children dress like children around the world, in comfortable, casual clothes.

Dress

Most Greeks wear modern clothing like people in the United States and Western Europe. But for festivals and national holidays, some Greeks enjoy wearing traditional costumes, especially during Greece's national holidays.

The *foustanella* is the official uniform of Greece's Presidential Guard in Athens. It consists of a skirt (kilt), white shirt, and embroidered woolen vest. A sash is worn around the waist. Shoes with pompons on the top complete the costume.

Greek women whose husbands have died often wear long black dresses and black scarves. Usually they wear these garments during forty days of mourning. But in many villages, Greek women wear black for years after the death of a family member.

A Greek village woman wears a traditional black dress and headscarf.

The foustanella was first worn by Greek soldiers during the 1821 revolution.

Olive orchards stretch for miles over the rolling Greek countryside.

Exports

Olive orchards cover the hills of the Greek countryside. Greece is the third-largest producer of olives in the world. High-quality virgin olive oil is a healthy part of the Greek diet and is also a major export.

Feta cheese is made from the milk of sheep and goats. Greece is the world's largest producer and exporter of feta cheese. Both feta cheese and olive oil are key ingredients in Greek salads.

MEDITERRANEAN GREEK SALAD

WHAT YOU NEED:
- 3 cucumbers, seeded and sliced
- 1 1/2 cups crumbled feta cheese
- 1 cup black olives, pitted and sliced
- 3 cups diced plum tomatoes
- 1/3 cup diced sun-dried tomatoes, packed in olive oil; drain and save the oil
- 1/2 red onion, sliced

HOW TO MAKE IT:
In a large salad bowl, toss together the cucumbers, feta cheese, olives, plum tomatoes, sun-dried tomatoes, 2 tablespoons of the saved sun-dried tomato oil, and the red onion. Chill in the refrigerator until you are ready to serve.

Food

Greeks love to eat salads with their meals. Mediterranean Greek salad can be made in about ten minutes and serves eight. Ask an adult to help you make Greek salad using this recipe.

Government

The government of Greece is a parliamentary republic. Greek citizens elect three hundred deputies to the **parliament.** The Greek parliament is called the *Vouli.* Two-thirds of the deputies must elect the president, who serves a five-year term. But the president does not rule the country. Instead, he appoints a prime minister from the strongest party in the Vouli. This prime minister works with the Vouli to lead the Greek government.

The Vouli meets in a beautifully restored palace that is called the Parliament Building. The building was constructed during the mid-1800s as a palace for King Otto. Greece stopped having kings in 1974.

**Greek president
Karolos Papoulias**

History

An ancient marble bust of Alexander the Great

Greece is often considered the birthplace of Western Civilization. Some 2,500 years ago, Greeks developed the philosophies and politics that led to modern democracy. Greek art, poetry, and science gave rise to Western culture and learning.

Alexander the Great may have been the most influential man in Greek history. Alexander was born in 356 B.C. in Macedonia. He was handsome, athletic, and a fierce warrior. Many historians believe he was the greatest military genius of all time.

At the time of his death, Alexander had conquered much of the known civilized world. He took Greek ideas and culture to the places he conquered. Alexander the Great helped build the foundation of Western Civilization.

Socrates

Important People

Greece has been the home of some of the world's greatest thinkers and writers. Although they lived more than two thousand years ago, their ideas are still studied today.

Plato

Homer

The philosopher Socrates was born in 469 B.C. Socrates taught his students to think critically about the best way to live their lives. He was totally committed to seeking the truth.

Plato was a student of Socrates. He was born in 427 B.C. Plato's most famous writing is titled *The Republic.* In *The Republic*, Plato discusses the nature of justice, wisdom, courage, and moderation.

Aristotle was born in 384 B.C. He studied logic, ethics, physics, and politics. Aristotle was Plato's student and became Alexander the Great's teacher.

Homer was a legendary Greek poet. His two epic poems are the *Iliad* and the *Odyssey.* These exciting story-poems have been read for centuries all over the world.

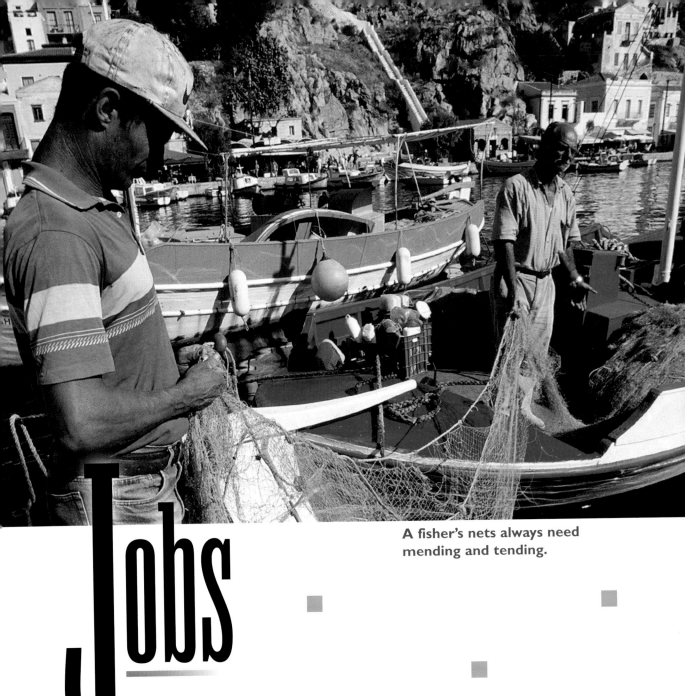

A fisher's nets always need mending and tending.

Jobs

More than 60 percent of all Greek workers are employed in service jobs. Many work in the tourist industry. Greece attracts some 15 million tourists each year!

Thousands of farmworkers care for olive orchards. Shepherds care for large flocks of sheep and goats. The seas surrounding Greece provide plenty of jobs for people who fish.

Keepsakes

Visitors to Greece can find beautiful **replicas** of items from ancient times. Two of the most popular keepsakes are gold jewelry and pottery.

Today's goldsmiths are very skilled. They make exact replicas of bracelets, earrings, and necklaces from Greece's past.

Greek potters use the same red clays that ancient potters used. They shape the clay into pots, vases, and plates. Figures of ancient gods and warriors are painted on the surfaces in precise detail.

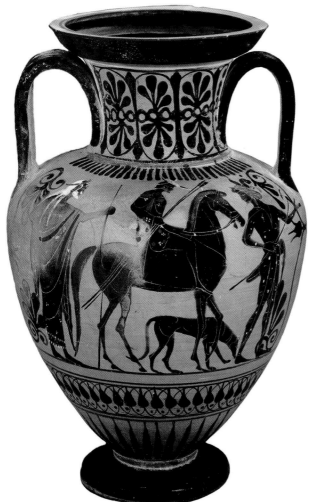

Reproductions of pottery like this sixth-century B.C. vase are popular keepsakes for tourists.

Greek goldsmiths are famous for their fine handiwork. This bracelet is decorated with beautiful gold serpents.

17

Land

Greece is a land of rugged mountains and brilliant blue seas.

Greece is one of the most mountainous countries in Europe. The country also includes a large number of islands in the **Aegean** and **Ionian** seas.

In Greek mythology, Mount Olympus is the home of the gods.

More than 60 percent of Greece's land surface is covered by mountains. Mount Olympus is the highest peak at 9,570 feet (2,917 meters). In the winters, the high mountains are covered with a blanket of snow.

No part of Greece is much more than 50 miles (80 kilometers) from the sea. And Greece has more than 2,000 islands, making up roughly one-fifth of its area. The Greek Islands, which are surrounded by stunning turquoise-blue waters, are one of the world's major tourist destinations.

BULGARIA

THE FORMER
REPUBLIC OF
MACEDONIA
(FROM)

ALBANIA

Mount Olympus
9,570 ft. (2,917 m)

GREECE

Aegean
Sea

TURKEY

Ionian
Sea

★ Athens

Map

Samaria
Gorge ▪

Rhodes

Crete

Nation

The official flag of Greece is blue and white. The blue represents the sky overhead and the seas that surround Greece. The white represents freedom and purity of heart.

A white cross is located in the upper left-hand corner of the flag. This symbolizes the Greek Orthodox religion. The nine blue-and-white stripes represent the Greek motto. There is one stripe for each syllable in the motto *Eleutheria H Thanatos* (eh-lef-the-RI-A EE THA-nah-tos). It means "Freedom or Death."

The Meteora Rocks

Only in Greece

The Meteora Rocks of Greece are **unique** geological formations. They rise above the plains of northern Greece. These "rock forests" average 1,000 feet (305 m), but some reach nearly twice that high!

Meteora

(meh-teh-OR-rah) means "high in the air" in Greek

Originally, monks reached these clifftop monasteries by retractable wooden ladders or by being hauled up and down in nets lifted by winches.

During the eleventh century, **hermit** monks began to occupy the tops of the rock formations. Eventually, they built twenty-four **monasteries** on the peaks. The monks constructed large **winches** to haul building materials up the vertical walls.

Today, only six of the monasteries survive. They have become popular tourist sites. The Megalo Meteoro Monastery contains the Church of the Transfiguration, with its beautiful murals and statues.

Greeks are proud of their
long history and rich heritage.

People

There are few ethnic minorities
in Greece. Ninety percent of the
nation's population is Greek.

Tourists and locals alike enjoy Greece's many sidewalk cafés.

The Greek people love to meet in sidewalk cafés. They enjoy socializing over a cup of very strong coffee. Many Greeks take siestas (afternoon naps), especially during hot summer months, and stay up late at night.

In cities, people live in crowded apartments and small houses. Many Greek parents build a house for each of their daughters and their families. On the islands, most of the houses are painted totally white.

Gleaming white houses cover many of Greece's steep hills.

Bouzouki music is enjoyed throughout Greece.

Question What is a bouzouki?

A bouzouki (boo-ZOO-kee) is a stringed instrument used to play traditional Greek music. Old-style bouzoukis have three sets of double strings. Modern bouzoukis have four sets of double strings. The sound box is small and shaped like a pear. The neck of the instrument is long and narrow.

Musicians claim that the bouzouki is the most difficult stringed instrument to play. Years of practice are required to play well. Greeks say that they want to jump up and dance when they hear the music of a bouzouki.

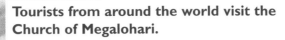

Tourists from around the world visit the Church of Megalohari.

Orthodox Greek Monastery

Religion

Almost all Greeks are members of the Greek Orthodox Church. Christianity can trace much of its early history to Greece. Greek Christians believe that the Apostle John wrote the Bible's Book of Revelations on the Greek island of Patmos.

Greek Orthodox churches and monasteries dot the landscape of Greece. The Church of Megalohari is the nation's most important pilgrimage site. Inside the church is an **icon** of the Virgin Mary. Many pilgrims believe that the icon will grant healing powers through prayer.

27

School for Greek children is the same as for children most everywhere.

School & Sports

A free public education is available to all children in Greece. The law requires students between the ages of six and fifteen to attend school. Most students ride buses or walk to their neighborhood school.

Soccer is the most popular sport in Greece. There are several professional soccer teams. Basketball and volleyball are growing in popularity. Almost all Greek children learn to swim when they are young.

A Greek soccer championship game

At high speeds, hydrofoils lift the body of this boat completely out of the water.

Transportation

Athens has a new subway system called The Metro. It can move 140 million passengers a year! The Metro has helped reduce car traffic and air pollution in the city.

Ferries and **hydrofoils** carry thousands of passengers to the Greek Islands every day. Greece also has one of the largest merchant navies in the world. Large Greek merchant ships deliver freight to countries around the globe.

The Samaria Gorge is on the island of Crete.

Unusual Places

The Samaria Gorge is a spectacular site in the White Mountains on the island of Crete. The gorge is almost 10 miles (16 km) long. Vertical rock walls rise 1,000 feet (305 m) from the floor of the gorge. At its most narrow point, called the gates, the gorge is only 10 feet (3 m) wide.

The gorge has become a popular tourist attraction for hikers. On most days, about three thousand hikers test their physical skills in the gorge.

The Theater at Epidaurus was built almost 2,500 years ago and is still in use today.

Visiting the Country

Archaeological sites are considered by many people to be the crown jewels of Greece. Ruins of ancient Greek civilization are scattered across the mainland and islands. The United Nations has identified sixteen World Heritage Sites in Greece.

Some of the more popular sites are the Acropolis, the Temple of Apollo, and the Theater at Epidaurus. The Theater at Epidaurus was built in the fourth century B.C. It is shaped in a semicircle with fifty-five rows of stone seats. It originally could seat twelve thousand to fourteen thousand spectators. Much of the theater has been restored and is being used today.

The stadium at Delphi

Window to the Past

The first Olympic competition was held in Olympia, Greece, in 776 B.C. There was one event, a 200-yard (183-m) foot race.

**The Olympics had their start in ancient Greece,
more than 2,700 years ago.**

In ancient times, the Olympics were held every four years.
New events such as wrestling, boxing, long jump, and discus
and javelin throw were added as time passed.

The Olympics were banned at the end of the fourth
century A.D. In 1896, the modern Olympics were established.
They were held at the Panathenaic Stadium in Athens, the site
of ancient competition.

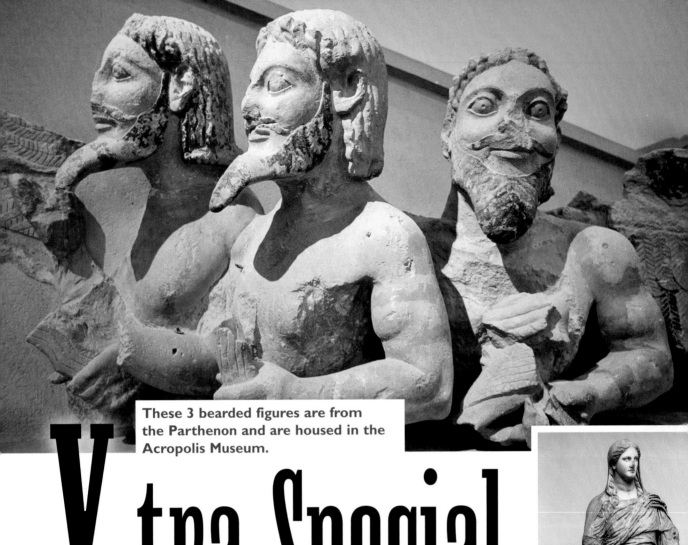

These 3 bearded figures are from the Parthenon and are housed in the Acropolis Museum.

X-tra Special Things

The Elgin Marbles are in the British Museum in London.

Many Greeks believe that the British should return the Elgin Marbles to Greece.

Greek goddess Athena

The Parthenon is a beautiful marble temple in Athens. It was built more than two thousand years ago to honor Athena, the Greek goddess of wisdom. Once, the Parthenon held many marble sculptures and statues. Today, they are part of an international **controversy**.

In 1801, a British man named Lord Elgin removed some of the marble works from the Parthenon. He had received permission to do this from the Turkish rulers who controlled Greece at that time. Lord Elgin then sold the artwork to the British government.

The collection of sculptures and statues is now on display in the British Museum. Many people believe these national treasures should be returned to Greece.

Greek Easter celebrations are joyous, yet solemn events.

Yearly Festivals

You can find a festival almost every day of the year somewhere in Greece. Some festivals celebrate religious holidays. Others celebrate historic events.

Ochi

(OH-hee)
means "No!" in Greek

Many children wear traditional costumes and wave Greek flags to celebrate Greek Independence Day.

Greek Orthodox Easter is the most important festival in Greece. Many Greeks attend a candlelight mass at midnight to begin their Easter celebration.

Greek Independence Day is celebrated on March 25. This celebration honors the War of Independence from the Turks, which began in 1821.

Ochi Day festivities occur on October 28. On this day in 1940, during World War II (1939–1945), the Greeks refused to let invading Italian troops pass through their country.

Delicious pastries are served on Greek Easter and other national holidays.

37

Zeus

Zeus is the king of the gods in ancient Greek **mythology**. His home is on top of Mount Olympus. Zeus rules the world with total power. His brother Poseidon rules the sea. Another brother, Hades, is the ruler of the underworld.

Zeus is feared by everyone. His symbol is a lightning bolt. Zeus uses the lightning bolt as a weapon of destruction. Mortal men try hard not to offend this powerful god.

Mighty Zeus, king of the gods in ancient Greek mythology, controls the weather as well as upholds law and justice.